HEART'S VOYAGE

MICHEAL M. DELAMOUR

ISBN 979-888569880-1

This book is dedicated to Veronica.

Contents

1. Story of Michael and Veronica

It all started when my father decided to send me to study at a Catholic high school in a suburb of Baguirmi province located thousands of kilometers from the capital N'Djamena. I was so devoted to the well-done job that I spent almost all of my time reading novels and doing house exercises while others were interested in cultural activities such as dance, theater.

My life and my daily activities were going on calmly and discreetly until this evening when our high school received a new student from the South-West zone of the country. She seemed lovely and dapper... She was probably one of those girls to give joy, hope to others. One of those rare stars who are very friendly with everyone and whose smile turns hot tears into laughter.

In addition to these qualities, that girl was a mastermind; she understands the lessons in the fastest way that she suddenly became my competitor in the classroom since I had never had one before.

But what happens practically?

Every Saturday, we have intellectual debates with the elders that we claim that being more experienced than us, we could learn a lot of good morals and stories from them. But there was a Saturday, I don't remember the date but instead of having the debate, we had the fellowship meal to welcome the new students who arrived on campus; After this meal a discussion took place between the part of the ambassadors of peace, our elders and the revolutionaries of the technological era, we. It was a cynical talk and we touched on minute subjects.

From those conversations, I realized that I was not just dealing individually but as a duo; not with me alone but also with another in me; that I was not only taking care of myself or my personality only but that of an unknown personality that drains a great strength from me.

So my results were going downhill. And until this moment of the life of an inexperienced boy in life, I didn't know what was haunting my mind.

The only thing that always comes to my mind is that of this new student who arrived who joined a few weeks ago.

I drew in my head its rounded forms, in addition to its sonorous and too fine voice which asks relevant questions to the teachers and without forgetting this approach which sometimes attracts my attention and distracts me during lessons. VERONICA was that girl that I was describing, yes Veronica is her first name, and I praise her so much because she seemed to be a different human being than I had ever met in my life. She taught me things I didn't believe in life even though we had never had a head-to-head discussion. I saw in her a strong girl, who, alongside a man, will be the reason for his success, his dedication to success, and his inspiration.

And I was still looking for the solution to my problem, eventually, my habits and schedules changed and it became hard to get my previous life back.

How could a person also have a significant influence on my life?

How will I get out? These are questions that come to mind every time.

Every night before sleep takes me, I was only imagining the plans and ways to face Vero but the reality was I even lose control of myself and became stupid in front of this creature so much that my mouth could not come out to declare this flame which burned me from within... I was so cowardly that I got angry with myself.

I could not understand the essence of what is going on in me. Several of my teachers questioned me to find out if I would have a family palaver or whatever was the reason for my sudden change. And I always replied. That everything is fine and that I will get back to work.

The negligence was home to me, the tenacity that animated me disappeared, and everything became done with all my actions were nonchalant. In these moments, I had seen the need to have a friend, a confidant who would be there to reboot my memory, bring me back to reason since I was derailing but I had no friend. I was that kind of boy who, solicitude was part of every day and that meditations and readings are part of it.

And I still remember the discussions we had with my parent,

that one was my model and my person, he is the direct and concrete relationship with life and its troubles and problems; it's one of the rarest I've had in my life because we didn't have the chance to live together as son and father. I have neither benefited nor learned from his immense wisdom, from this complete knowledge of the traditions and customs of the Ngam society which is mine, something that I regret. My parent said to me and I quote: 'The reality could in one or another, or even in most part be very different from your dreams or your expectations but to have a human character, it is to be ready to find resolutions to the countless challenges of life or at least to brave them with stubbornness and relentlessness. The diligent attachment to a decision oh that's what it's all about.

And these words are strong in meaning, they are enough to spur me on and embolden me to push high this capacity for reflection and to use my brain to solve my enigmas.

Months went by and time passed very quickly as the end-of-year exams were already looming on the horizon. Our teaching of natural sciences had given us work to do in groups on the causes, effects, and possible solutions to the phenomenon of global warming and the mechanism of the greenhouse effect. Oh! How lucky! The breakdown put us in the same group with Vero, and can you guess the feeling that was rumbling inside me? It was no doubt a feeling of satisfaction, joy, jubilation; I was voluptuous because the opportunity to speak is finally there. I understood that day the words of my math teacher who stipulated: the feeling of pleasure, of windfall, never lasts; besides, it's just like a feeling of crush in love which is similar to fireworks, you have to seize it at any moment to rejoice in it, you'll never be in seventh heaven and this taste for being in angels will be missed forever. I saw that my teacher's intuition and lucidity were not treacherous but truthful.

After the classes, as the group leader of our presentation, I announced the meeting in the evening so that I could dot the i's and get our work ready for the presentation itself.

At the indicated time, all the members of the group were present;

We talked for a long time, we didn't seem to get along, oh yes! That's the idea of the work, everyone wanted to be heard and have their opinion applied. I had to do my job as leader of the group, bring people to order, and take everyone's ideas and efforts into consideration, which is fair because the spirit of the team wants it that way.

The agendas were over and we had to go our separate ways; everyone was going their way and me having an agitated mind wanting to leave, suddenly, I heard myself calling from behind: Michael,

Nonchalantly I faced the person who had called out to me and I saw Vero;

I had become speechless, yes in front of me is Vero, this angelic person who seems to be another me. She was in a black dress and on her feet a blue vans shoe and wearing a black jacket. I took courage and spoke to her.

I asked her how she was doing, and she answered me in a quiet and a little melancholy voice: I'm alright and I want to go home with you. She came to hold my hand and started asking me tons of questions about myself, my family…It looks like a court interrogation.

This evening was unforgettable of my life.

I was happy that day, will I always be? Reality might have something else in store for me, but I didn't care about the rest, the most important thing is that I am happy at this moment in life.

Michael and Vero walked hand in hand like people who have a deep relationship; Vero was telling me about her family, how she holds herself to study, and her short and long-term plans. She asked me a question that took me a few minutes without answer, it was this: Michael why did you never approach me? Don't know that we can make things impeccable together?

I kept silent and looked towards the sky, it was all blue and I saw from afar a group of crows flying from very far away and it was very beautiful to see, I invited Vero to contemplate this beauty and posed this question: are you able to see this innocent beauty of nature? I see she replied.

I dreamed that one day, you would be this blue sky, which is infinite in its size, and that I could be this group of crows that can fly to any side of this sky and make it even more beautiful in the eyes of the world.

Did I answer your questions Vero? Somehow but you're hard

to understand. What do you practically mean Michael?

You are the one that all you have to do is smile and my day is won, you are mystical Veronica, you made me forget who I am, where I was, and a large part of my past.

It was a huge thing for you that the dimensions were insufficient for it to come out, and it weighed on me all the time my mouth couldn't untie to explode it.

She was completely silent and seemed surprised while listening to all these words…

And I believe that nothing is strange to you in all that I have just said, I continued.

Here you are today and well in front of me and I believe that I will return with one of the greatest memories of my life.

Vero was still silent and kept giving me a melancholy look with his eyes that were bathing in tears.

Why shed Vero tears? Do you want me to shed guns too? You know I just don't want to see you girl, and if it gives you that feeling then I'm desperate about it I sighed in her ears;

It was after these words that I saw the girl open her mouth and want to talk to me, she was indeed candid and ingenious that I felt guilty at that moment.

Michael, don't you know that one is sublime and transcendent when one is reckless to fight for what one loves? She quoted Maytouza LeNgamaboy to me in this sense: <The will, is felt in the faculty of associating all our forces and powers for what is wanted, otherwise, it is envy>

Oh, it seemed to be an intellectual battle between her and me, harder than stronger.

Vero I say, you never knew it but know that solitude was my route, Yes Vero my childhood and my school life happened in the whirlwind of this atmosphere, hence my taciturn but blessed nature is this evening.

I never knew I could stand up to that brainer girl. I always doubted my strengths and powers but I found myself magical and full of talent and charisma that night.

Vero looked at his watch and said to me: oh Michael the campus will be closed soon, I have to go back and we will discuss this matter tomorrow but know that I am happy to listen to you and I firmly believe that we will face the difficulties together.

She kissed me on the cheek and left. I stood there watching Vero leave; I couldn't say a single goodbye to her.

When she reached the gate to their campus, she turned and met my gaze, smiled, and waved her hand in a sign of goodbye.

Pretensions are not always obvious I told myself, and I went there to devote myself to my nocturnal occupations as planned in my schedule.

The night of this evening was unique, a night of a deep breath, of insightful thought, of an unprecedented dream, of shrewd imagination.

I was only constantly re-listening in my mind to this cavernous and bewitching voice of the young girl. I could in no way erase a single word from her sentences. Thus I spent one of the unforgettable nights of my life that night. I got all the reasons to be happy, I felt like the happiest in the world because the person who's my world cared about me, she was attentive and devoted to talking to me; I thought I am of the greatest people in this world. I there knew something important about Life, I understood that the love and concern of our beloved people is the starting of happiness; it is all about responding yes to who else needs.

The following day, in the evening, I felt bored so I decided to go to the doom ground of my high school to see the students who were preparing performances for the prom event and; when I came, Vero was there with her friends; I joined the boy Team at the entrance gate, they were a dance team but they knew I couldn't do anything dancing was one of my weakness. Vero left her friends and came and took me asked my teammate if she could have a word with me, demand granted! I noticed that cinema, reading, walks in nature, these were our common hobbies; Music, I like it, but my shyness had prevented me from learning to dance, but the paradox is that I was a good singer, who even won first prize for best slammer that year. We wanted to go for a stroll but because Vero is an organizer of the event, we couldn't and thus we couldn't even finish our previous discussion. We knew and saw a need of talking to each other but we could at that time. She is called to her duties.

I think my first dance step, I did it at a prom of year. God, how stiff and ridiculous I was! I believed all eyes fixed on me and it paralyzed me. I was ashamed of my Awkwardness. Still, Vero was gently dragging me away. You know, Vero I'm not a star dancer...

I didn't need to tell her. She was well aware of it, the poor girl, so did I step on her toes. It does not matter, you will learn very quickly, I am certain.

I would like to dance at the Say (local dance of the Ngam community), you know! She smiled at me, moved closer to me and I felt the soft touch of his body. And said, you'll take me to your city one day that we'll dance say it. Is not it?

Yes. You will see how comfortable I am at home. Over there I am in my element. I believe that I am a boy who can only be at ease in the urban environment which saw me born.

After those words, the girl was called on the campus; Michael I want to have time and talk to you but I am sorry I have to go, we will meet tomorrow she said. We gave a deep hug to each other, I hugged her so tight that we didn't want to part.

I watched her leave. A force enveloped me, I became suddenly sad, and one would say that I sensed that besides this simple goodbye was hiding a farewell. I couldn't see Vero going that way. It was as though I knew I will never see her again, my body felt the feeling of weakness, I couldn't stand up on my legs because they became so soft and without strength.

What I felt around Vero were amazing well-being, a feeling of peace in the soul, and the inexplicable body. And I felt that Vero was one of those rare young people, daughters who are for the man a compliment, support.

I went home and spent a so long night thinking of us, thinking about Vero and me when I listened obstinately to a voice telling me: you have a long day at work so you have to rest to wake up strong but when I looked at the alarm stuck to the wall of my room, it was 5 AM, and time to get ready for classes.

I showered, had my dinner, and headed to school. Indeed I will have to cross the main street to reach the school because this street separates the campus and the buildings of the school itself;

As usual, I looked on both sides of the street and crossed, suddenly, a motorcyclist was coming in the opposite direction, at a considerable speed, the time that I turned around to suspect the noise of the machine which seemed to be coming towards my direction, I tumbled and found myself on the ground, the pileup was painful and catastrophic in such a way that I fainted.

I'm not sure what happened to me but thanks to prayers and my loved ones I woke up on the bed of Claron Health International Hospital.

I had a broken left leg, a fractured right hand, wounds all over my body, and eye problems that require operations by an eye surgeon.

From time to time, I was cured but unfortunately, I could not write my end-of-year exam because of my state of health.

I had thus lost contact with my classmates; what happened to my Vero? No answer to this question and life took a heterogeneous and unknowing turn.

2. MY LIFE TOOK A TURN OF PRANKS

From N'Djamena, I found myself in Accra, and I knew nothing about all that. When I opened my eyes, I saw my mother by my side, this strong woman was there alongside her son, looking morose and sullen and when she met my gaze, she shed tears;

I couldn't look at my mama a second time, my tears flowed. How sad! She gave me birth but never thought of what could happen to me; she always wishes me good without thinking that the worst thing could happen to her son as well.

She never had the idea that after I was born, and that means I am from that time exposed to the joy and sadness of the world; that I became, from the day of my birth, a component of nature and that I could not escape the plagues that constitute it.

I couldn't at that moment but I heard my mama telling me what happened to me and how we had traveled for my care.

The greatest of sentences fell to me that day when my parents decided that I should stay in Accra to continue my studies, I felt my world ended like this, I did not have to start another story and a new one again, I was aimless, asthenic, and decay defined my new person. Even when I tried to stand up, my legs could hardly support my entire body, and it occurred to me that on the day of doomsday; this is how those who are unprepared will feel.

I took courage and gave myself back to life because I read in the book "the young people ask themselves", volume 2 that <despair is like the clouds, and the clouds always end up dissipating>; These words were enough for me to heal my pain and that one day I will find a Veronica.

3. MEETING VERONICA

A few weeks ago, I was returning from my classes at my faculty and I saw at a distance a girl who was used to wearing black and who had her hair tied together, which was not braided;

For me, it's Vero and not someone else but as I was at a significant distance, she went away and I couldn't see her.

I did everything to see her but virtually undone for days.

That girl is indeed Veronica's identity, her incarnation, her direct similarity without leaving the shape, the eyes, and the way of reasoning and speaking;

So I was in a hurry to meet her and get to know her, but it was not easy.

I have trouble and it hurts my self-esteem when I realize that the person for whom our destinies were linked does not have the slightest attention, concern for me but it was someone other than Vero, it is that I completely forgot.

And what a coincidence! The new person I just confused Vero with is called Veronica.

It's from there that God does so many things that he created Vero exactly as I dreamed.

Veronica, can you assimilate this? Was it a cumshot?

I don't know absolutely anything about it but I need you, it's the most of the sensations that passed me by, need to talk to you, to listen to you, to discover you, to know you because I don't know the answer, nor the reason why but I feel like my ideal person;

it's true and it's a fact that we don't know enough apart from the somatic portrait, but believe me, the greenness and the energy of what I hold within me is more vigorous than it ignores everything else.

You may think that I am violating the law of the majority which states that "feelings are based on a broad knowledge of a person's strengths and weaknesses" but also know that this majority omits that love should also be born from a reason to be captivated and seduced, from a well-founded good reason or from that one that we do not know.

You, you are the ideal person who could appear in my existence as spiritual support, the guarantor of my joy. My infatuation with you has grown over time and you seem to be everything else.

One fine morning while I was reading my bible, I arrived at 1 corinthians13:4-8, then I understood later that I was on the yoke of a heavyweight and this weight weighs down because it is not only based on physical attractiveness but precisely on what it must build and take root in.

Yes, I keep thinking that the most difficult exercise is to get someone to think and see things your way because we have different perceptions and analogies but the most important thing is to get a result eloquent and tangible.

The greatest chimera that I no longer want to fall into is to inhibit my empathy to the detriment of navel-gazing reason.

Nature would have wanted things according to the biotic components of which you are apart.

You know what, I was so radiant to have a conversion with you during this evening, and it taught me to thin out that you are an attentive and spontaneous person.

Tonight Vero, your eyes in the glasses had the same sparkles as Vero.

I was there watching you speak, and immersing myself in a world that I smelt from afar but never had the chance to taste.

Vero, you can only know intentions and my personality when you are near me. I can see this uniqueness and fantasy of you and me.

We can conceive, plan and succeed all together by this force that binds me to you.

He is strong and can bear anything above all else, he craves to carve himself and push even deeper.

The disappointments of life but the most important thing is to discern what is good for you.

If the child should also suffer or pick up the knock-snaps for the misunderstandings or blunders of the parents then the world would be meaningless and the land of plenty would have a considerably limited numeric and limbo a vast majority of that number.

This is why it would be better and even improved if the predecessors were not palisades for the unsuspected.

You ended up becoming my whole universe, I felt so connected to you that it is unimaginable for me to think that you could be what I believe or what I expect of you.

All I would like is for you to be a part of my story and I yours, the one who can help me, to guide my thoughts, to comfort me, you are for me a subject of encouragement, of hope in times of challenges and vice versa because I see in you this strength capable of doing it, this energy of a strong and unique girl.

I indeed want it intimate and sincere because my difficulties will always be braved as long as you're there.

Victor Hugo, whom I much prefer, said :<< the feeling that embodies the other in us is to be two buts and to be only one. A male and a female who merge into an angel, that's heaven>>.

To see it real and apparent, this magnetic thought of being immersed in this extra world of you, this universe of the duo which could form the uniqueness of us is the desire of the soul of my personality and my spirit.

One of the most difficult exercises that I believe I have encountered in my way of thinking is the fact of being able to infiltrate the life of others who are unaware of your existence, of what you are for them or you could create in them. , and seek to gain their trust.

Sometimes nothing lasts or nothing has its place to exist for the simple reason that we haven't left space for it to grow and take root; we don't consider it because of bad experiences and failed attempts... Or for so many personal reasons, I whispered to myself.

Was that real life? Should I give up what I'm doing for people's lack of attention or lack of support? If so then I'm a worthless coward, absolutely pathetic, I say to myself, yes absolutely obsolete... Because we have lots of colors in life, each person likes one or even several colors; some colors are made based on others and this is exactly a picture of life, it has a multitude of colors; different faces at different times and you know what will make you distinguished? It is to apply, starting at the local level, your way of thinking, and to scaffold. I ask myself too many questions and this imaginary world is the best that can help me resolve my concerns.

The resolution is that there are thousands or even an uncountable number of things in life to discover every day of our life and that we must be curious and brained to unmask them and bring them to light. In this case, we would have to accept life as it saw us born and conceive of it in our humble and adorable manner; I say to myself.

4. WORDS AND VERBS ,VERBS EXTERNALIZE THE EMPATHY IN ME

You know what Vero?
the most beautiful thing that I dream of is to be
with you, tell you about them
finest of stories; make you hear
and live the beat from my heart.
I imagine us only two by the sea
Contemplating the wonders of nature
I watch us hugging each other
I watch myself lose in your lively and
alluring gaze The image of your small
shape similar to that of a gazelle can't
leave my mind; Veronica, words can't
take it perfectly this joy in me which
waters and floods my heart personality
is fair the ideal of My incarnation little princess.
You are like a tree and me the birds of the sky;
their life remains forever doomed
and their relationship and not
become indelible.

so I could eat your fruits relying on

you in time of fatigue and distress.

You are comparable to a young

pigeon and me the dove,

I'll get you the best of me to see you upright,

I will cover you with my

wings against the coolness

and against winds and tides.

You have a singular and charming look;

Like the moon at the bottom of the lake that

reflects her, your pupil, where shines a wet spangle,

At the corner of your sweet eyes rolls languidly;

They seem to have taken his diamond fires;

They are of finer water than a perfect pearl,

And your great eyelashes moved, with their restless wing,

Only half-veil their vivid radiance.

A thousand little loves, in their mirror of flame,

Could to look and find themselves more beautiful there,

And desires go there to relight their torches.

They are so transparent, they show your soul,

Like a celestial flower with an ideal chalice

That we would see through a crystal.

Hope to dream the good

Your beautiful eyes make me want

To see you and see what I appreciate

In you, I want to be a knight Veronica

To see you is to scream

This silence created by your universe

Who enchants me with pretty verses?

So stay like that, eyes fixed

I want to breathe and be asphyxiated

By your air enriched and so pure

I want your feeling so sure

About me by your gaze

And even if you close your eyes

From you, I only feel better Veronica.

I see you as another me, you are my

Mirror, through you, I see your future

A brighter future. I write to you

words

I write you to express the feelings in me

I write you my happiness I draw it on your lips

I describe my life to you I dedicate you

my heart so far from you my life is full of misfortunes

I offer you my nights I offer you my days

I offer you my soul I offer you, my love

with my poems, I invent a kingdom for you

I will create our empire to protect you

my princess so that you live in me and me in you.

You are a flower necklace held by my tears

you are a tear lost but which survived you invent in my heart

the definition of the word happiness I draw you in my memory

as my goddess of hope, I write to you with the ink of my

heart.

I stayed for quite a while in darkness

He was so calm and today I want you to know

My angel soft fragile

What feelings!

My heart could explode with joy.

I could watch you and your eyes

Gently set me apart you are

so happy that your adorable skin,

so soft and shiny makes me want to caress it.

I want you if you knew

How much I care about you

How much you are needed

In my life, you wouldn't dare

Not to miss a single one

Moment, you would always stay

Near me your soul

against my soul and heart to heart…

Love is sometimes

want to despise

but not to gossip.

To love is sometimes to have

the feeling of being alone

to understand certain things,

try timidly to share,

do not impose, then be silent.

To love is to listen,

watch, try
to perceive the subtle.
Loving is over the days,
seize the opportunity
to enlarge his heart.
To love is to give of love selflessly
To love is to try is to respect.
To love is to see the child in every person.
To not have complicated happiness.
To love is sometimes to receive
a divine kiss of well-being,
the soothing breath of an angel over his being.
To love is to be small and big at the same time.
To love is to perceive sunbeams
in the apparent darkness feelings.
To love is to have the heart
filigree printed under his thoughts
To love is often detect the solitary gaze
on the other looking for happiness
behind bars from his inner prison.
To love is to have the heart
pure and light and,
like the painter, gently add
here and there a few touches
of colors in the paintings of life.
Love is sometimes to be nervous
and anger, but it is mostly

know how to smooth out the waves
storms of his heart.
To love is sometimes to see a slanderer
and shed a tear compassionate
on his dryness of heart.
And I didn't choose you but I fell on you,
nature offered me to you,
You do not cease to occupy this place in me.
It's all been in my heart girl.
It's just you and me, Veronica.

5. COULD WE FLY HIGHER TOGETHER VERONICA?

Can you get in there and give your best for him young girl?

Can you share this flow of energy that can cause such a reasonable, strong motion but which above all, can be watched by decay when it fails?

How can two people appear in my life, in identical conditions?

And can if I don't take into account the physical similarity because they say, each person has his image or the person who is similar to him somewhere in the world;

I keep leaning on other characters to ask myself, why do they have the same pseudonyms, why this nominal convergence of Veronica?

And how to behave as the same as how to act?

Is this a coincidence? And if that's the case, why did I, who was another being, completely different, meet them at the same time and in the same life circumstances?

I don't have any answers to my questions but all I conclude is that there are things that fate can link, maybe that's part of it;

Life brings people together and separates them not because they choose but the occurrences have them intimately.

Believe young incredible divine creature that you are part, yes of this story which is mine and yours, of our story and we can write it together by considering our experiences and formulating a definition for the hours that remain to us.

Can't you imagine, we can gaze into infinity and join forces to transcend barriers no matter how grandiose they could be?

I have this curiosity to discover and know and I can undoubtedly conclude that Veronica defines in one way or another the person whom I have just met. How can one claim to know the person one has just met? It may seem paradoxical but in truth, I knew her, so long ago, I lived and shared with her.

You are the one who needs lots of affection to feel good about yourself. Your displayed confidence and the distance you create around you send a message that does not correspond to you. Deep down, Veronica, you are certainly modest, but more shy than haughty. You have difficulty feeling comfortable and will have a hard time trusting someone. You rarely confide your feelings. you are demanding with those around you, which greatly destabilizes the people around you, especially at first. You like to make decisions and have a great sense of analysis, which makes you a tough competitor at work. Besides, no one takes you lightly, professionally, your natural authority makes you formidable in everyone's eyes, and you command, respect, and never let yourself go. You seem to know perfectly well how to differentiate between her professional life and your private life, which gives you a considerable advantage and strength.

Can you give me your hand so that we can believe in it and set in motion a concretized form of intuitions and flair which could be ours?

What do you think of us?

Are you blind in the way that you can't see what my eyes see?

What if we decide together to go and make it happen?

I have a poem for you Vero, it's so short but full of meaning, it might be a travel word and the passport that will take us to the destined country:<<if your heart loves my heart as my heart loves your heart and let the two-beat for each other, our two hearts will beat in chorus>>.